# LinkedIn Edge: The Ultimate Guide to Successful Marketing Strategies on LinkedIn

B. Vincent

Published by RWG Publishing, 2023.

While every precaution has been taken in the preparation of this book, the publisher assumes no responsibility for errors or omissions, or for damages resulting from the use of the information contained herein.

LINKEDIN EDGE: THE ULTIMATE GUIDE TO SUCCESSFUL MARKETING STRATEGIES ON LINKEDIN

**First edition. May 2, 2023.**

Written by B. Vincent.

# Table of Contents

# Chapter 1: Introduction - Why LinkedIn is Essential for Your Marketing Strategy

Over 740 million people from more than 200 countries and territories are connected through LinkedIn, making it the most extensive professional networking platform in the world. It presents a one-of-a-kind opportunity for companies and professionals to connect with one another and grow their brands in a manner that is both highly targeted and highly efficient.

In this chapter, we will discuss why using LinkedIn as part of your marketing strategy is important, as well as how the platform can assist you in achieving your business objectives.

To begin, LinkedIn offers a possibility for business-to-business marketing that is unequaled. You will be able to communicate with a highly specific group of business professionals through the use of this platform. This audience includes decision-makers, influencers, and thought leaders. Your marketing efforts can be targeted based on factors such as job title, company size, industry, and geographic location, which increases the likelihood that your message will be received by the appropriate individuals.

Second, the social networking website LinkedIn is a potent instrument that can be used to establish and cultivate relationships with customers, prospects, and peers in the industry. You can establish yourself as a thought leader among your audience and build trust and credibility with them if you share content that is of value to them, participate in meaningful conversations, and join relevant groups.

Thirdly, LinkedIn provides a variety of advertising options, such as sponsored content, sponsored messaging, and display ads, which enable you to communicate with the members of your target audience in a manner that is highly relevant and individualized.

The last benefit of using LinkedIn is that it gives you access to a wealth of data and analytics, which enables you to monitor and improve the effectiveness of your marketing efforts. You are able to monitor your engagement rates, click-through rates, and conversion rates by using the insights provided by LinkedIn. You can then make use of this information to modify your strategy and gradually improve your results.

In a nutshell, your marketing strategy cannot exist without LinkedIn for the following reasons:

It presents a one-of-a-kind opportunity for B2B marketing, giving you the chance to communicate with a highly specific group consisting of business professionals.

It is an effective instrument for establishing and maintaining relationships with customers, prospects, and colleagues in the same industry.

It provides a variety of advertising options, enabling you to communicate with the members of your target audience in a manner that is highly pertinent and individualized.

It gives you access to a wealth of data and analytics, which enables you to evaluate and improve the effectiveness of your marketing campaigns.

You are passing up a significant opportunity to connect with your target audience, establish yourself as a thought leader, and drive business growth if you are not already using LinkedIn as part of your marketing strategy. If you are not using LinkedIn, you are missing out. In the following chapters, we will delve into the topic of maximizing the potential of LinkedIn to accomplish your marketing objectives in a more in-depth manner.

# Chapter 2: Understanding Your Audience - Identifying and Targeting Your Ideal Customers on LinkedIn

Understanding your target demographic is one of the most important factors in the success of your marketing efforts on LinkedIn. You can make certain that your marketing efforts are highly targeted, personally tailored, and successful if you first determine who your ideal customers are and then target them.

In this chapter, we will discuss the key steps that you need to take in order to understand your audience and target the customers who are the best fit for your business on LinkedIn.

Step 1: Define your target audience

The first thing you need to do is determine who your ideal customers are. Who are the individuals on LinkedIn whom you hope to connect with and engage in conversation with? Think about things like your job title, the industry you work in, the size of your company, where you live, and your interests.

LinkedIn offers a variety of targeting options, such as job function, seniority, company size, industry, and more, in order to assist you in defining the audience that you wish to communicate with. Make use of these options to create audiences that are extremely relevant to the marketing campaigns you are running.

Step 2: Carry out the necessary research

The next step is to carry out research in order to gain a better understanding of your intended audience. Where do they struggle the most, what are their biggest challenges, and what do they want most? On LinkedIn, what kinds of posts do they like to comment on and share? When they are not at work, what are some of their interests and hobbies?

In order to carry out research, you have access to a wide variety of tools and resources, such as LinkedIn Insights, Google Analytics, and research reports compiled by third parties. In addition, you can collect information and feedback from your target audience by having them participate in interviews, focus groups, and surveys.

Step 3: Develop buyer personas

You will be able to develop buyer personas, which are detailed profiles of your ideal customers, once you have a solid understanding of the demographics of your target audience. Information such as a buyer's job title, responsibilities, and challenges, as well as their goals, interests, and buying behaviors, should be included in a buyer persona.

You can make marketing campaigns that are more targeted and personalized by developing buyer personas. These campaigns will be able to speak directly to the requirements and interests of your audience.

The fourth step is to develop content that is targeted.

At long last, you have the ability to produce targeted content that directly addresses your ideal customers. Make sure that your content strategy is guided by your buyer personas by developing content that addresses their pain points, provides answers to their questions, and provides value.

Articles, videos, infographics, and other forms of media are just some of the different types of content that can be found on LinkedIn. Make use of a variety of presentation methods to keep your content interesting and up to date.

In conclusion, if you want your marketing efforts on LinkedIn to be successful, it is critical to first gain an understanding of your audience and then zero in on your ideal customers. You can ensure that your marketing efforts are highly effective and drive business growth by defining your target audience, conducting research, developing buyer personas, and creating targeted content. These steps are all part of the inbound marketing methodology.

# Chapter 3: Crafting Your Personal Brand - Optimizing Your LinkedIn Profile for Maximum Impact

―――

Your online personal brand is represented by your LinkedIn profile. It is your chance to make a good first impression, to demonstrate your skills and expertise, and to bring in new opportunities for business.

In this chapter, we will discuss the essential steps that need to be taken in order to maximize the impact of your LinkedIn profile.

Identifying your personal brand is the first step.

The first thing you should do is articulate your personal brand. What is your unique value proposition? How do you differentiate yourself from the other people in the room? Think about the areas in which you excel, the areas in which you have the most experience, and the areas in which you have the most knowledge.

You can define your personal brand by conducting a SWOT analysis, which involves identifying your strengths, weaknesses, opportunities, and threats. You can then use this information to develop the messaging and positioning of your brand.

Create an attention-grabbing headline as the second step.

When someone visits your LinkedIn profile, the very first thing that catches their attention is your headline. It is of the utmost importance to craft a captivating headline that accurately reflects your personal brand and catches the attention of the audience you are aiming to connect with.

Your headline ought to be succinct, unmistakable, and centered on the advantages that you have to offer the people reading it. Increase your visibility in search results by including keywords that are pertinent to both the field in which you operate and the audience that you intend to attract.

Step 3: Improve the effectiveness of your summary section

You have the opportunity to highlight your personal brand and provide an overview of your skills and areas of expertise in the summary section of your LinkedIn profile. Tell your story, highlight your accomplishments, and demonstrate your worth by utilizing this section of the application.

Make sure to include keywords and phrases that are pertinent to your business and the people you are trying to attract as customers. Maintain a conversational tone and stay away from using overly technical language or jargon specific to your industry.

Step 4: Emphasize your previous work experience and educational attainment.

Establishing your credibility and demonstrating your level of expertise requires a strong showing from your experience and education sections of your resume. Be sure to include all experience and education that is pertinent, including any certifications or awards you may have received.

When you are describing your experience, rather than focusing solely on your job responsibilities, emphasize the accomplishments and results you have obtained. Make use of numbers and statistics to demonstrate your value and quantify the impact you have had.

Step 5: Embellish your profile with various forms of multimedia.

Your profile on LinkedIn can include a variety of multimedia components, such as images, videos, and documents, if you choose to include them. Make use of these components to improve your profile and display your work more effectively.

Include, for instance, a video introduction of yourself, a portfolio of your work, or examples of projects that you have completed in the past. Make use of these components to illustrate your level of expertise and to present a more all-encompassing picture of your personal brand.

To summarize, optimizing your LinkedIn profile is essential for building your personal brand and attracting new business opportunities. You can find more information on how to do this here. You can ensure that your LinkedIn profile stands out and leaves a long-lasting impression on your target audience by defining your personal brand, composing an enticing headline, optimizing your summary section, highlighting your experience and education, and using multimedia to enhance your profile.

# Chapter 4: Creating Content that Engages - Best Practices for Writing and Sharing Effective Posts on LinkedIn

---

Creating and disseminating content that is of value to your audience on LinkedIn is one of the most effective ways to engage that audience. Establishing yourself as a thought leader and gaining the trust and credibility of your target audience can be accomplished through the provision of valuable insights, information, and other resources.

In this chapter, we will discuss the most effective ways to write and share posts on LinkedIn, as well as the best practices currently available.

Step 1: Determine who you are speaking to.

The first thing you need to do is get to know your target demographic. Which types of content do they feel best meet their needs? What kinds of things do they have an interest in? Your content strategy should be guided by your buyer personas as well as the research you did on your audience.

When you are developing content, you should concentrate on subjects that are pertinent to both your sector and the people you intend to reach. Maintain a conversational tenor and steer clear of overly technical language as well as jargon specific to your industry.

Step 2: Create valuable content

The content that you share with your audience on LinkedIn ought to be of benefit to that audience. It should educate, inform, or entertain them, as well as provide insights or solutions to the problems or difficulties they are experiencing.

Think about utilizing a variety of content formats, such as articles, infographics, videos, and polls, and make sure to use a combination of these formats so that your content remains interesting and up-to-date.

Step 3: Use engaging headlines

When people come across your content on LinkedIn, the very first thing that they see is the headline you've chosen to use. It is critical to write headlines that are compelling and attention-grabbing at the same time.

Use numbers, statistics, and questions in your headlines to pique your audience's interest. When highlighting the benefits of your content, be sure to make use of impact words like "proven," "effective," and "game-changing," among others.

Step 4: Include visuals

Visuals can help to make your content more engaging and shareable. Some examples of visuals include images, videos, and infographics. Use visuals to illustrate your points, provide context, and add interest to your content.

Be sure to employ high-quality visuals that are pertinent to the content you're sharing and that resonate with the people you're trying to reach. Make use of captions as well as alt text in order to supply additional context and improve accessibility.

Optimize your profile for LinkedIn's algorithm, which is the fifth step.

The algorithm that powers LinkedIn decides which pieces of content users see in their feeds and how frequently they see it. It is absolutely necessary to optimize your posts for the algorithm in order to increase the likelihood that your content will be seen by others.

You can increase the visibility of your posts by including relevant hashtags and keywords in your posts. Improving engagement can be as simple as choosing the right format for your content, such as video or text. Additionally, you should post frequently in order to raise your visibility and build momentum.

Developing and disseminating content that is of value to your audience is absolutely necessary in order to engage them on LinkedIn. You can create effective posts that drive engagement and build your personal brand on LinkedIn if you know your audience, create valuable content, use engaging headlines, include visuals, and optimize for LinkedIn's algorithm.

# Chapter 5: Building Your Network - Strategies for Connecting with the Right People on LinkedIn

G rowing your personal brand, expanding your reach, and building relationships all require that you establish a robust network on LinkedIn. But because there are more than 740 million people using the platform, it can be difficult to connect with the appropriate individuals.

In this chapter, we will discuss the most effective methods for establishing connections with the appropriate individuals via LinkedIn.

Step 1: Define your target audience

The first thing you need to do is determine who your ideal customers are. Who are the individuals on LinkedIn that you would like to connect with and why? Think about things like your job title, the industry you work in, the size of your company, where you live, and your interests.

Make use of LinkedIn's search function as well as its advanced filter options to locate individuals who satisfy your requirements. You can also find potential connections by using the company pages, events, and groups on LinkedIn.

The second step is to customize your invitations.

When sending invitations to connect with others, it is critical to personalize the messages that you send. Do not simply send a generic invitation; instead, take the time to craft a personalized message in which you explain why you want to connect with the recipient and how you can add value to the interaction.

Be specific about the reasons you want to connect with each other and the ways in which you can assist one another. You could, for instance, bring up a common interest, line of work, or connection between the two of you.

Engage with your network as the third step.

After you have established a network for yourself, maintaining regular contact with the people you have met through it is an absolute necessity. Like and comment on the posts they make, share the content they produce, and make contact with them in order to begin conversations.

Building relationships, establishing trust and credibility, and keeping yourself in people's minds all require active participation in your network. Because your engagement will show up in the feeds of your connections, it will also help to increase the amount of people who can see you on the platform.

Step 4: Take the initiative.

Be proactive in the process of building your network rather than waiting for people to come to you. Make an effort to connect with people whom you hold in high esteem or who you believe could add something of value to your network.

You can also search for potential connections by using the "People Also Viewed" feature that is available on LinkedIn. This function displays the profiles of other users who are comparable to the person whose profile you are currently viewing. Utilizing this function is an excellent way to make new connections with people who have similar interests to your own.

Step 5: Provide value

Last but not least, it is critical to add value to the connections you have made. Share content that is of value, provide insights and recommendations, and be generous with both your time and your expertise.

By giving your network something of value, you not only help to build trust and credibility with them, but you also encourage them to interact with you and share your content with their own networks.

Building a solid network on LinkedIn is essential if you want to grow your personal brand and increase the number of people who are exposed to your work. You can construct a network of connections who can assist you in accomplishing your professional objectives by identifying your target audience, personalizing your invitations, actively engaging with your network, being proactive, and providing value to others.

# Chapter 6: LinkedIn Groups - How to Use Them to Boost Your Visibility and Credibility

———

The ability to build relationships, demonstrate your expertise, and broaden your reach on LinkedIn can all be accomplished through participation in groups on the platform. Through participation in groups, you can make connections with other professionals who have similar interests, share content that is of value to others, and demonstrate your expertise.

In this chapter, we will discuss how to make the most of LinkedIn groups in order to increase both your visibility and your credibility on the platform.

Step 1: Find relevant groups

The first thing you should do is look for relevant groups that you can join. Search for groups that are pertinent to your line of work, your areas of interest, and the people you intend to reach. Make use of LinkedIn's search function as well as its advanced filter options to locate groups that satisfy your requirements.

When evaluating groups, it is important to take into account a variety of factors, including the size of the group, the level of participation, and the quality of the information that is exchanged.

Step 2: Participate in discussions

After you have become a member of a group, it is imperative that you take part in the conversations that take place there. Leave comments on the posts, talk about what you know and what you've learned, and ask questions.

Establishing your expertise, cultivating relationships with other members of the group, and raising your profile on the platform are all made easier when you take part in group discussions.

Step 3: Distribute Useful Material to Others

In addition to taking part in the conversations taking place, it is imperative that you also contribute content that is of value to the group. Disseminate any articles, blog posts, and other forms of content that are pertinent to the concerns of the group.

When you share content with others, be sure to include a concise summary as well as your own thoughts and observations on the reasons you believe the content to be valuable. This helps to start a conversation and encourages other members of the group to engage with the content that you have shared.

Step 4: Conduct yourself in a respectful and professional manner.

When interacting with members of other groups, it is critical to maintain a respectful and professional demeanor at all times. Steer clear of contentious subjects or conversations that could be interpreted as inciting hostility. Maintain an upbeat and encouraging manner in your communication.

Always keep in mind that the LinkedIn groups you participate in are professional forums, and that your actions will reflect on both your personal brand and your credibility.

Step 5: Form your own independent organization

In conclusion, if you are unable to find an appropriate group to join, you should think about initiating your own group. Building relationships with other professionals who share similar values and interests enables you to cultivate a community centered on your particular areas of interest or expertise.

When beginning a new group, it is important to have a firm understanding of the group's mission and objectives, and to invite people whom you believe may be interested in taking part. Prepare yourself to devote some of your time and energy to guiding the group's discussions and moderating the gathering.

In a nutshell, the groups that you participate in on LinkedIn are an effective method for increasing both your visibility and your credibility on the platform. You can establish yourself as a thought leader and build relationships with other professionals in your industry by searching for relevant groups, participating in discussions, sharing valuable content, being respectful and professional, and starting your own group.

# Chapter 7: LinkedIn Ads - Maximizing Your ROI with Targeted Advertising Campaigns

———

L inkedIn Ads are an effective method for reaching your desired demographic, spreading awareness of your brand, and fueling the expansion of your company. You are able to create highly targeted campaigns that get results thanks to the advanced targeting options and analytics offered by LinkedIn.

In this chapter, we will discuss ways to increase your return on investment (ROI) by using targeted advertising campaigns on LinkedIn.

First, you'll need to define the objectives of your campaign.

The first thing you need to do is determine the objectives of your campaign. What do you hope to accomplish with the advertising campaign you are running? Do you want to raise people's awareness of your brand, generate leads, or drive traffic to your website?

You can create campaigns that are specifically designed to achieve those goals, and you can measure the success of your campaigns against those goals, if you first define your goals and then write them down.

Step 2: Target your audience

LinkedIn provides a variety of targeting options that enable you to connect with potential clients for your business. Your target audience can be narrowed down based on a variety of factors, including job function, seniority, company size, industry, and more.

Create highly targeted audiences that are more likely to interact with your advertisements by using your buyer personas and audience research as a guide for your targeting strategy.

Step 3: Construct Ad Content That Is Compelling

The content of your advertisements is extremely important if you want to attract the attention of your target audience and encourage engagement. Develop compelling advertising content by focusing on the positive aspects of your product or service and speaking specifically to the issues that your target audience experiences and struggles with.

Make your advertisements stand out from the crowd by including captivating visuals like photos or videos. Make sure the messaging you use is direct and to the point, and that it emphasizes the value of the product or service you offer.

Optimize your ad targeting and bidding, which is the fourth step.

It is essential to continually optimize your ad targeting and bidding in order to get the most return on investment (ROI) from your LinkedIn Ads. Experiment with a variety of targeting options and different approaches to bidding to determine which methods produce the best results.

Make use of the analytics and reporting tools provided by LinkedIn to keep track of how well your advertisements are performing, and then make any necessary changes to further improve their effectiveness.

Step 5: Keep an eye on your campaigns and make necessary adjustments.

Last but not least, it is essential to monitor and adjust your campaigns on a consistent basis. Always keep a close eye on key performance indicators, such as click-through rates, conversion rates, and cost per conversion.

Make adjustments to certain targeting options or ad content in order to improve the performance of those elements if you find that they are not performing as well as you had hoped. In a similar vein, if you discover that particular targeting options or ad content is doing exceptionally well, you should devote a greater portion of your budget to developing those facets of your business.

In conclusion, LinkedIn Ads are an effective method for reaching one's intended audience and fostering the expansion of one's business. You can maximize the return on investment (ROI) of your LinkedIn Ads and accomplish your business goals if you first define the goals of your campaign, then identify your audience, then create compelling ad content, then optimize your ad targeting and bidding, and finally monitor and adjust your campaigns.

# Chapter 8: LinkedIn Analytics - Measuring and Analyzing the Performance of Your LinkedIn Marketing Efforts

———

It is essential to measure the performance of your LinkedIn marketing efforts in order to understand what aspects of your strategy are producing positive results, what aspects are not, and how you can improve your results. The analytics tools offered by LinkedIn provide insightful information regarding the performance of your company's content, advertisements, and overall marketing strategy.

In this chapter, we will discuss how to measure and evaluate the effectiveness of your marketing efforts on LinkedIn.

Step one: Determine your objectives and key performance indicators (KPIs).

Establishing your objectives and key performance indicators (KPIs) is the first thing you should do. What do you hope to accomplish with the help of your marketing efforts on LinkedIn? How will you measure your progress and what metrics will you use?

KPIs for LinkedIn marketing typically include engagement metrics like likes, comments, and shares, as well as conversion metrics like clicks, leads, and website visits. Other common KPIs for LinkedIn marketing include views, connections, and recommendations.

Use LinkedIn Analytics as the second step.

LinkedIn Analytics gives you access to a wide variety of tools that you can use to evaluate the effectiveness of your marketing initiatives. Utilize these tools to track your progress in relation to your goals and key performance indicators (KPIs), and to identify areas in which you can improve.

You could, for instance, track the performance of your posts by using LinkedIn Analytics. This would allow you to monitor engagement metrics such as the number of likes, comments, and shares, in addition to reach and impressions. In addition, you can use LinkedIn Analytics to monitor the effectiveness of your advertisements, including the number of clicks, impressions, and conversions.

Step 3: Analyze your data

When you have collected data using LinkedIn Analytics, the next step that is absolutely necessary is to analyze that data in order to recognize patterns and obtain insights. Keep an eye out for patterns in your data, such as increases in user participation or shifts in conversion rates.

Make use of this information to determine areas that could be improved upon and to make adjustments to your strategy. For instance, if you notice that particular categories of content are generating more engagement than others, you can modify your content strategy so that it focuses more on the categories of content that are generating the most engagement.

Step 4: Put your content through an A/B test.

A/B testing is a powerful tool that can help you optimize the marketing efforts you put into LinkedIn. You can determine which variations of your content produce the best results by conducting experiments with a number of distinct permutations of your content, such as a variety of headlines, images, or calls-to-action.

You can optimize your posts, ads, and landing pages with A/B testing, and base your decisions regarding your marketing strategy on the results of these tests.

Step 5: Iterate and improve in a consistent manner.

In conclusion, it is essential to iterate frequently and improve your LinkedIn marketing efforts in order to be successful. Make changes to your strategy based on the insights that you glean from LinkedIn Analytics so that you can get the best possible results from your efforts.

Try out a variety of content formats, targeting options, and ad formats, and make use of A/B testing to improve the effectiveness of your campaigns over time.

In conclusion, it is essential to understand what aspects of your LinkedIn marketing are working, what aspects are not working, and how you can improve your results by measuring and analyzing the performance of your LinkedIn marketing efforts. You can maximize the effectiveness of your LinkedIn marketing efforts and achieve your business goals by setting goals and key performance indicators (KPIs), utilizing LinkedIn Analytics, analyzing your data, A/B testing your content, and continually iterating and improving your strategy.

# Chapter 9: Leveraging LinkedIn Company Pages - Building and Growing Your Company's Presence on LinkedIn

———

C ompany pages on LinkedIn are an effective resource for developing your company's brand, engaging with your ideal customers, and propelling business expansion and growth. You can increase the amount of people who see your content on LinkedIn and establish your business as a thought leader in your field by establishing and maintaining a robust company page on the platform.

In this chapter, we will investigate how to make the most of LinkedIn company pages in order to construct and expand the presence of your company on LinkedIn.

Create an engaging profile for your company as the first step.

The first thing you need to do is develop an engaging company page that exemplifies your brand and draws attention to the products or services you offer. To make your page stand out from the crowd, incorporate high-quality visuals like pictures and videos.

Include in-depth information about your company, such as its mission and values, its history, and your history. To increase the number of people who find your page through a search engine, include industry-specific keywords and phrases in its content.

The second step is to distribute useful content.

When you have finished creating your company page, one of the most important things you can do is share useful content with your audience. Distribute articles, blog posts, and other forms of content that are pertinent to the interests of your target audience as well as the industry in which you operate.

Make sure to include a concise summary of each piece of content, as well as your own thoughts and observations on the reasons why you believe it to be valuable. Make your content more engaging and shareable by incorporating visuals into it.

Engage with your audience in the third step.

It is essential to build relationships and establish your credibility on LinkedIn, and one of the best ways to do this is to engage with your audience. Quickly respond to people's comments and messages, and get involved in the conversations taking place in LinkedIn groups.

Utilize the analytics tools that LinkedIn provides to keep track of how well your content is performing and adjust your strategy accordingly. For instance, if you notice that particular categories of content are generating more engagement than others, you should modify your content strategy so that it focuses more on the categories of content that are generating the most engagement.

Step 4: Use LinkedIn Ads

LinkedIn Ads can assist you in reaching out to your ideal customers and driving growth for your company. Make use of

LinkedIn's targeting options to get your ads in front of the right people, and develop compelling content for your ads that emphasizes the positive aspects of the products or services you offer.

Utilize A/B testing to optimize your advertisements over time and increase your return on investment (ROI). Utilize LinkedIn's analytics tools to keep an eye on how well your advertisements are performing, and if necessary, make changes to improve how well they are doing.

Step 5: Measure your results

Last but not least, it is critical to monitor the outcomes of your LinkedIn company page and adapt your strategy accordingly. Tracking engagement metrics, such as likes, comments, and shares, as well as conversion metrics, such as clicks and leads, can be accomplished with the help of the analytics tools provided by LinkedIn.

Make adjustments to your strategy in light of the insights that you obtain from analyzing your data in analytics. For instance, if you notice that particular categories of content are generating more engagement than others, you should modify your content strategy so that it focuses more on the categories of content that are generating the most engagement.

In a nutshell, it is absolutely necessary to make use of LinkedIn company pages in order to construct and expand the presence of your company on the platform. You can establish your company as a thought leader in your industry and drive business growth on LinkedIn by creating an engaging company page, sharing valuable content, engaging with your audience, using LinkedIn Ads, and measuring the results of your efforts.

# Chapter 10: Showcasing Your Products and Services - Best Practices for Creating and Sharing Engaging LinkedIn Showcase Pages

———

Showcase Pages on LinkedIn are an effective method for showcasing the goods and services offered by your company and interacting with members of your target demographic who frequent the platform. You are able to create a unique page for each of your products or services through the utilization of Showcase Pages, where you can then share content that is particularly pertinent to the aforementioned offerings.

In this chapter, we will investigate the most effective methods for developing and publishing engaging LinkedIn Showcase Pages.

First, determine which of your products or services are your most important ones.

The first thing you need to do is determine which of your most important products or services you want to highlight on LinkedIn. Pick out the items or services that are especially pertinent to the people who make up your target audience and that you want to put the spotlight on.

Step 2: Create compelling content

When you have determined which of your products or services are most important to your business, the next step is to produce compelling content that highlights those products or services. Make your Showcase Pages stand out from the crowd by including high-quality visual content like images and videos.

Include specific information about each product or service, such as its characteristics and the advantages of using it. Make it easier for people to find your Showcase Pages by including industry-specific keywords and phrases in the content you publish there.

Engage with your audience in the third step.

It is essential to build relationships and establish your credibility on LinkedIn, and one of the best ways to do this is to engage with your audience. Quickly respond to people's comments and messages, and get involved in the conversations taking place in LinkedIn groups.

Utilize the analytics tools that LinkedIn provides to keep track of how well your content is performing and adjust your strategy accordingly. For instance, if you notice that particular categories of content are generating more engagement than others, you should modify your content strategy so that it focuses more on the categories of content that are generating the most engagement.

Step 4: Use LinkedIn Ads

Using LinkedIn Ads can assist you in reaching your target demographic and fostering business expansion for your most important products and services. Make use of LinkedIn's targeting options to get your ads in front of the right people, and develop compelling content for your ads that emphasizes the positive aspects of the products or services you offer.

Utilize A/B testing to optimize your advertisements over time and increase your return on investment (ROI). Utilize LinkedIn's analytics tools to keep an eye on how well your advertisements are performing, and if necessary, make changes to improve how well they are doing.

Step 5: Measure your results

Last but not least, it is absolutely necessary to evaluate the outcomes of your Showcase Pages and adapt your strategy accordingly. Tracking engagement metrics, such as likes, comments, and shares, as well as conversion metrics, such as clicks and leads, can be accomplished with the help of the analytics tools provided by LinkedIn.

Make adjustments to your strategy in light of the insights that you obtain from analyzing your data in analytics. For instance, if you notice that particular categories of content are generating more engagement than others, you should modify your content strategy so that it focuses more on the categories of content that are generating the most engagement.

In a nutshell, LinkedIn Showcase Pages are an effective method for displaying the goods and services offered by your business and communicating with members of your target demographic who frequent the platform. You can establish your company as a thought leader in your industry and drive business growth for your key offerings by determining which of your products or services are the most important to your company, producing content that is compelling, engaging with your audience, using LinkedIn Ads, and measuring the results of these efforts.

# Chapter 11: Recruiting on LinkedIn - Strategies for Attracting Top Talent and Building a Strong Company Culture

———

L inkedIn is not only an effective platform for marketing and networking, but it is also a useful resource for finding new employment opportunities. Companies have the ability to connect with top talent and build a strong company culture by leveraging the extensive network of professionals that LinkedIn provides.

In this chapter, we will discuss strategies for recruiting top talent on LinkedIn, including building a strong company culture and attracting top talent.

1. Define your company's reputation as an employer

Establishing your employer brand should be your first priority. What is it about your company that makes it such a great place to work, and what values does it uphold? Your company's culture and values should be reflected in your employer brand, and it should distinguish itself from the brands of other businesses operating in your industry.

Make use of LinkedIn's Company Page and Career Pages in order to promote your employer brand and draw attention to the values and traditions of your business. You can give potential candidates an idea of the culture of your company by sharing photos and testimonials from current staff members.

Step 2: Use LinkedIn Recruiting Tools

You can connect with top talent on LinkedIn through the use of a variety of recruiting tools that are available on the platform. You can search for and get in touch with potential candidates by using LinkedIn Recruiter, and you can advertise your open positions to a large audience using LinkedIn Job Posts.

Utilize the targeting options provided by LinkedIn to communicate with prospective candidates based on their qualifications, job titles, and locations. Make use of the analytics tools provided by LinkedIn to monitor how successful your job postings are, and adapt your approach accordingly.

Encourage employee referrals as the third step

The use of employee referrals is an effective method for cultivating a robust company culture and drawing in top-tier candidates. Reward your employees for successful referrals of friends and coworkers to your business, and encourage them to refer their own friends and colleagues as well.

Make it simple for employees to recommend their personal networks to your business by giving them access to the Referral option on LinkedIn. Showcase the many positive aspects of working for your company by publishing success stories regarding employee referrals on your Company Page.

Engage with Potential Candidates as the Fourth Step

When it comes to developing relationships and establishing the credibility of your company on LinkedIn, engaging with potential candidates is absolutely necessary. In a timely manner, respond to messages and inquiries, and participate in the conversations taking place in LinkedIn groups.

Make use of the messaging tools provided by LinkedIn in order to connect with prospective candidates and begin a conversation with them. By providing potential candidates with content that is of value to them, your company can demonstrate its expertise and earn their trust.

Measure Your Results as the Fifth Step

In conclusion, it is essential to evaluate the outcomes of your recruitment efforts and modify your strategy in accordance with the findings. Tracking engagement metrics, such as views and clicks, as well as conversion metrics, such as applications and hires, can be accomplished with the help of the analytics tools provided by LinkedIn.

Make adjustments to your recruitment strategy in light of the insights gained from analyzing your data in the area of analytics. For instance, if you notice that certain job postings are generating a greater number of applications than others, you should modify your strategy for posting jobs so that it focuses more on the types of jobs that are generating the most interest.

In a nutshell, using LinkedIn as a recruiting platform is an effective method for luring the best possible candidates and developing a robust corporate culture. Build a powerful team of top talent and establish your company as a great place to work by defining your employer brand, using the recruiting tools on LinkedIn, encouraging employee referrals, engaging with potential candidates, and measuring the results of your efforts.

# Chapter 12: LinkedIn Sales Navigator - How to Use the Platform to Generate Sales Leads and Increase Revenue

The LinkedIn Sales Navigator is a powerful tool that can help increase revenue on the platform as well as generate sales leads. You are able to target the appropriate individuals and businesses with the help of Sales Navigator's sophisticated search and lead generation tools. These tools enable you to narrow your focus on specific aspects such as a person's job title, location, and other pertinent factors.

In this chapter, we will discuss how to utilize LinkedIn Sales Navigator to increase revenue and generate sales leads.

Step 1: Define your target audience

The first thing you need to do is determine who your ideal customers are. Who are the decision-makers in the companies that you have identified as potential clients, and what are their job titles and areas of responsibility? Utilize the advanced search tools provided by Sales Navigator to narrow down your search for the appropriate individuals based on their job title, location, and any other pertinent criteria.

Constructing a list of prospective customers is the second step.

After you have determined who your ideal customers are, the next step is to compile a list of potential customers. Utilize the lead generation tools provided by Sales Navigator to compile a list of prospective clients based on the criteria you've specified.

You have the option to save the results of your search and set up alerts that will inform you whenever new leads are found that match the criteria you specified. You can also expand your prospect list by importing the data pertaining to your current customers who are already enrolled in Sales Navigator.

Engage with prospective customers as the third step.

Building relationships and establishing your credibility on LinkedIn requires that you actively participate in conversations with prospective clients. Make use of the messaging tools provided by Sales Navigator to connect with prospective customers and start a conversation with them.

By providing potential customers with content that is of value to them, your business can demonstrate its expertise and earn their trust. Utilize the InMail feature of Sales Navigator to send personalized messages to prospective customers, and track your messages to see who among your recipients has opened and engaged with your messages.

Step 4: Keep an eye on how far you've come.

Sales Navigator gives you access to a wide variety of analytics tools, which allow you to monitor how effectively your lead generation efforts are working. Make use of these tools in order to track your progress in relation to your goals and determine areas in which you can improve.

Keep track of both the metrics that measure engagement, such as views and clicks, and the metrics that measure conversion, such as leads and revenue. Make adjustments to your strategy for lead generation based on this information in order to achieve the best possible results.

Step 5: Use LinkedIn Ads

Increasing your revenue and connecting with your ideal customers can both be accomplished with the assistance of LinkedIn Ads. Make use of the targeting options provided by Sales Navigator to ensure that you are communicating with the appropriate individuals, and develop compelling advertising content that focuses on the advantages offered by your goods or services.

Utilize A/B testing to optimize your advertisements over time and increase your return on investment (ROI). Use the analytical tools that come with Sales Navigator to keep an eye on how well your advertisements are performing, and if necessary, make changes to improve how well they are doing.

In a nutshell, LinkedIn Sales Navigator is a potent tool that can increase revenue on the platform while also increasing the number of sales leads generated. You can establish your company as a thought leader in your industry and drive revenue growth on LinkedIn by defining your target audience, building a prospect list, engaging with potential customers, tracking your progress, and making use of LinkedIn Ads.

# Chapter 13: Maximizing Your LinkedIn SEO - Tips and Tricks for Optimizing Your Profile and Content for Search Engines

The use of search engine optimization (SEO) is essential in order to make your LinkedIn profile and the content you post there discoverable by the audience you are trying to reach. You can raise the amount of people who see your profile and content on LinkedIn as well as increase the amount of traffic that is driven to your page if you optimize your profile and content for search engines.

In this chapter, we will discuss various strategies that can help you improve the search engine optimization of your LinkedIn profile.

Step 1: Optimize your profile

Your first order of business is to fine-tune your LinkedIn profile. You can make it easier for people to find your profile by including the appropriate keywords and phrases in your headline, summary, and experience sections.

You can make your profile stand out from the crowd by including a professional profile photo and background image. Make use of the multimedia features offered by LinkedIn in order to upload images, videos, and documents that highlight your expertise and experience.

Step 2: Use relevant keywords in your content

When you're trying to optimize your content for search engines, using keywords that are relevant to the topic at hand is absolutely necessary. Make use of keywords and phrases that are pertinent to the field that you work in as well as the interests of your target audience.

You should include keywords in the titles, descriptions, and actual content of your posts. Utilize the tagging feature offered by LinkedIn to add pertinent tags to your posts. This will make your posts more discoverable to users who are looking for specific subject areas.

Step 3: Post content to your LinkedIn profile.

Increasing your visibility on LinkedIn and driving more traffic to your page can be accomplished by publishing content on LinkedIn, which is a powerful way to boost your visibility on the platform. Use the publishing platform that LinkedIn provides to share articles, blog posts, and other content that is pertinent to the interests of your target audience and the industry in which you operate.

Be sure to include pertinent keywords and phrases in the titles and descriptions of your posts, and make use of visuals to create content that is both more engaging and more able to be shared.

Engage with your audience, which is the fourth step.

It is essential to build relationships and establish your credibility on LinkedIn, and one of the best ways to do this is to engage with your audience. Quickly respond to people's comments and messages, and get involved in the conversations taking place in LinkedIn groups.

Utilize the analytics tools that LinkedIn provides to keep track of how well your content is performing and adjust your strategy accordingly. For instance, if you notice that particular categories of content are generating more engagement than others, you should modify your content strategy so that it focuses more on the categories of content that are generating the most engagement.

Step 5: Monitor your search engine optimization metrics

Last but not least, it is essential to monitor your SEO metrics and adjust your strategy in accordance with the data. Tracking engagement metrics, such as views, clicks, and shares, as well as conversion metrics, such as leads and revenue, can be accomplished with the help of the analytics tools provided by LinkedIn.

Make adjustments to your content strategy in light of the new understanding you've gained from analyzing your analytics data. Adjust your content strategy so that it focuses more on the keywords that are driving the most traffic to your profile or content, for instance, if you notice that certain keywords are driving more traffic than others to your profile or content.

In conclusion, optimizing your LinkedIn SEO to its full potential is essential if you want to raise your profile's visibility on the platform and attract a greater number of visitors to your page. You can establish yourself as a thought leader in your industry and drive more business growth on LinkedIn by optimizing your profile, using relevant keywords in your content, publishing content on LinkedIn, engaging with your audience, and monitoring your SEO metrics. Additionally, you can publish content on LinkedIn.

# Chapter 14: The Power of LinkedIn Recommendations - Leveraging Social Proof to Boost Your Credibility and Authority

Recommendations on LinkedIn are an effective method for establishing your credibility and increasing your authority on the platform. Recommendations provide social proof that you are a skilled and competent professional, and they can help you stand out in a competitive job market by helping you differentiate yourself from other applicants.

In this chapter, we will discuss the power of recommendations on LinkedIn and how to make the most of them to increase your credibility and authority in your field.

Step 1: Request Recommendations

The first thing you should do is send a request to your LinkedIn connections asking for recommendations. Make it a point to get in touch with colleagues, clients, and other professional contacts and ask them to recommend you with a letter of recommendation.

Be specific about what you want them to include in their recommendation, such as specific experiences or skills that you want to bring attention to, and give them clear instructions.

The second step is to make recommendations.

On LinkedIn, getting recommendations from other users is an effective way to build relationships and demonstrate your expertise in your field. You should highlight your colleagues' and clients' abilities and experiences in recommendations that you write for them and send them to other professional contacts.

Use LinkedIn's recommendations feature to request recommendations from your connections. Be specific about what you want them to include in their recommendation, such as specific experiences or skills that you want to bring attention to, and give them clear instructions.

Step 3: Exhibit Your Suggestions and Recommendations

It is imperative that you highlight the recommendations you have received on your LinkedIn profile once you have received them. Include the recommendations in your profile, and draw attention to them in the sections devoted to your summary and experience.

Make use of the multimedia features offered by LinkedIn to upload images or videos that highlight your expertise and experiences. Spread the word about your suggestions by posting them on other social media websites, like Twitter or Facebook, in order to get in front of more people.

The fourth step is to interact with the audience.

It is essential to build relationships and establish your credibility on LinkedIn, and one of the best ways to do this is to engage with your audience. Quickly respond to people's comments and messages, and get involved in the conversations taking place in LinkedIn groups.

Utilize the analytics tools that LinkedIn provides in order to keep track of how successful your recommendations are and to modify your approach as required. For instance, if you observe that particular kinds of recommendations are generating more engagement than others, you should modify your strategy so that it places a greater emphasis on those particular kinds of recommendations.

Step 5: Keep an Eye on Your Progress and Results

Last but not least, it is imperative to keep track of how your recommendations are working out in practice and adapt your strategy accordingly. Tracking engagement metrics, such as views and clicks, as well as conversion metrics, such as leads and revenue, can be accomplished with the help of the analytics tools provided by LinkedIn.

Make adjustments to your strategy in light of the insights that you obtain from analyzing your data in analytics. For instance, if you notice that certain recommendations are generating more engagement than others, you should adjust your strategy so that it focuses more on the types of recommendations that are generating the most engagement.

In a nutshell, recommendations on LinkedIn are an effective method for boosting your credibility and establishing yourself as an authority on the platform. You can establish yourself as a skilled and competent professional on LinkedIn and drive more business growth by requesting and giving recommendations, showcasing your recommendations, engaging with your audience, and monitoring your results. In addition, you can do this by showcasing your recommendations.

# Chapter 15: LinkedIn for Thought Leadership - Establishing Yourself as an Industry Expert and Influencer

———

LinkedIn is a powerful platform that can help you establish yourself as an expert in your field and an influential figure in your field. You can build your credibility and authority, and become a thought leader in your industry, by sharing content that is valuable to your audience, taking part in relevant discussions, and engaging with that audience.

In this chapter, we will discuss various methods for achieving thought leadership through the use of LinkedIn.

Step 1: Identify Your Particular Field of Specialization

The first thing you need to do is identify your specific area of expertise. Which subject areas excite you the most, and in which do you feel most confident sharing your knowledge? Utilize the search tools provided by LinkedIn to locate groups and discussions that are pertinent to your area of expertise, and then participate in these discussions to establish yourself as an authority in your field.

Step 2: Distribute Useful Content to Your Audience

When you want to establish yourself as a thought leader on LinkedIn, sharing content that others find valuable is absolutely necessary. Distribute articles, blog posts, and other forms of content that are pertinent to the interests of your target audience as well as the industry in which you operate.

Include your own personal observations and comments, and make use of visuals to create content that is not only more interesting but also easier to share. Utilize the tagging feature offered by LinkedIn to add pertinent tags to your posts. This will make your posts more discoverable to users who are looking for specific subject areas.

Step 3: Engage in Conversations and Debates

It is essential to take part in discussions on LinkedIn if you want to develop relationships with other users and establish your credibility on the platform. Quickly respond to people's comments and messages, and get involved in the conversations taking place in LinkedIn groups.

Make use of the messaging tools provided by LinkedIn in order to connect with other thought leaders in your field and begin a conversation with them. Build relationships with other users and establish your authority by sharing insightful perspectives and valuable insights, as well as by engaging with the content they create.

Displaying Your Thought Leadership Is the Fourth Step

Once you have established yourself as a thought leader, it is essential to showcase your thought leadership on your LinkedIn profile. This can be done by adding a section titled "Thought Leadership." You can highlight your expertise and share your insights and perspectives with potential employers by drawing attention to the experience and summary sections of your resume.

Make use of the multimedia features offered by LinkedIn in order to upload images, videos, and documents that highlight your expertise and experience. If you want to reach a larger audience, you should share the content you've created as a thought leader on other social media platforms like Twitter and Facebook.

Measure Your Results as the Fifth Step

Last but not least, it is imperative that you monitor the outcomes of your efforts to establish yourself as a thought leader and adapt your strategy accordingly. Tracking engagement metrics, such as views and clicks, as well as conversion metrics, such as leads and revenue, can be done with the help of the analytics tools provided by LinkedIn.

Make adjustments to your strategy for thought leadership based on the insights that you glean from the data collected by your analytics. For instance, if you notice that particular categories of content are generating more engagement than others, you should modify your content strategy so that it focuses more on the categories of content that are generating the most engagement.

To summarize, LinkedIn is a powerful platform that you can use to establish yourself as an expert in your field and an influential figure. You can establish yourself as a thought leader in your industry and drive more business growth on LinkedIn by defining your area of expertise, sharing valuable content, participating in discussions, showcasing your thought leadership, and measuring the results of your efforts.

# Chapter 16: Building a LinkedIn Content Strategy - Creating a Plan to Consistently Produce High-Quality Content

———

It is essential to have a content strategy for LinkedIn if you want to produce content of a high quality on a consistent basis, as well as increase your credibility and authority on the platform. You can establish yourself as a thought leader on LinkedIn and drive more business growth there by defining your content goals, determining your target audience, and developing a plan for the creation and distribution of content.

In this chapter, we will discuss different approaches that can be taken when developing a content strategy for LinkedIn.

First Step: Outline Your Content Objectives

The first thing you need to do is determine what your content goals are. What do you hope to accomplish with the content you create, and which metrics will you employ to evaluate how well you've done?

Increasing the awareness of your brand, generating leads for your business, and establishing yourself as a thought leader in your industry are all examples of content goals that could be pursued. Make use of the analytic tools that LinkedIn provides in order to monitor your progress in relation to your objectives and modify your content strategy as required.

Step 2: Determine Who Your Intended Readership Is

It is essential to identify your target audience before producing content in order to create something that will resonate with your audience and drive engagement. Who are your ideal customers, and what are the problems that they face and the things that they are interested in?

Make use of LinkedIn's search tools to locate groups and discussions that are pertinent to your business, and then participate in these discussions to gain a better understanding of the requirements and pursuits of your target audience. Make use of this information to guide the development of your content strategy and produce content that is pertinent to and beneficial for the audience you are trying to reach.

Create a Content Plan as the Third Step

The development of a content plan is an essential step in the process of producing content that is consistently of high quality. Use a content calendar to plan out your content for the upcoming weeks or months, identifying the topics and formats that you will use, and then use this information to create the calendar.

You might, for instance, intend to upload a new blog post to your website on a weekly basis or produce a series of videos centered on a particular subject. Utilize the analytics tools that LinkedIn provides in order to monitor how well your content is performing and make any necessary adjustments to your content strategy.

Produce Content of a High Quality as the Fourth Step

It is essential to produce content of a high quality if you want to establish yourself on LinkedIn as a thought leader and increase engagement with your profile. Make your content more interesting to read and easier to share by incorporating visual elements like photos and videos.

Include your own observations and comments, and make use of keywords and phrases that are pertinent to the topic at hand in order to optimize your content for search engines. Utilize the tagging feature offered by LinkedIn to add pertinent tags to your posts. This will make your posts more discoverable to users who are looking for specific subject areas.

The fifth step is to disseminate your content.

It is essential to distribute your content in order to communicate with your intended audience and encourage participation. You should publish your content on LinkedIn in addition to other social media platforms, such as Facebook or Twitter.

Engage in conversations taking place in relevant LinkedIn groups and make use of the messaging tools provided by LinkedIn to connect with other thought leaders working in your field. Utilize the analytics tools that LinkedIn provides to keep track of how well your content is performing and modify your distribution strategy as required.

Developing a content strategy for LinkedIn is essential if you want to produce content of a consistently high quality and position yourself as a thought leader on the platform. You can establish yourself as a thought leader in your industry and drive more business growth on LinkedIn by defining your content goals, identifying your target audience, creating a content plan, producing content of a high quality, and distributing your content. This can be accomplished through the use of content.

# Chapter 17: Collaborating on LinkedIn - How to Use the Platform to Connect and Collaborate with Other Businesses and Professionals

C onnecting with other businesses and professionals, as well as collaborating with them, is made easier through the use of LinkedIn's powerful platform. You can foster relationships, share knowledge, and propel the growth of your business through collaborative endeavors by taking advantage of the features offered by LinkedIn, such as its groups, messaging, and company pages.

Within the scope of this chapter, we will investigate various approaches to working together on LinkedIn.

Step 1: Join Relevant Groups

It is essential to join groups that are relevant to your industry if you want to find and connect with other businesses and professionals on LinkedIn. Make use of LinkedIn's search tools to locate groups that are pertinent to your line of work or areas of interest, and then join these groups to take part in discussions and exchange information with other users.

Be sure to add something of value to the conversation by discussing your own experiences and viewpoints, as well as taking an interest in the posts made by other users. Make use of the messaging tools provided by LinkedIn in order to connect with other users who are part of the group and begin a conversation with them.

The next step is to work together on the content.

On LinkedIn, one of the most effective ways to both share knowledge and build relationships is to work together on content projects. Creating a blog post or white paper together with another company or professional, for instance, is a great way to collaborate.

You can connect with potential collaborators and make a proposal to work together by using the messaging tools provided by LinkedIn. Be specific about what it is you hope to accomplish through the collaboration, as well as how each participant will benefit from it.

Step 3: Make Use of Your Company's Page on LinkedIn

The Company Pages on LinkedIn are an effective resource for fostering collaboration with other businesses as well as professionals. Make use of your company page to share updates and engage in conversation with other professionals and companies operating within your sector.

Utilize the analytics tools provided by LinkedIn to keep track of how users interact with your company page and make any necessary adjustments to your marketing approach. For instance, if you notice that particular categories of content are generating more engagement than others, you should modify your content strategy so that it focuses more on the categories of content that are generating the most engagement.

Participate in events hosted by LinkedIn. This is the fourth step.

It is absolutely necessary to take part in LinkedIn events in order to successfully build relationships with other businesses and professionals and to collaborate with them. Make use of the events feature on LinkedIn to locate events that are pertinent to your interests, such as webinars or conferences, and then participate in these events to network with other attendees.

Make use of the messaging tools provided by LinkedIn in order to connect with other attendees and begin a conversation with them. Be sure to share your own insights and perspectives, as well as engage with the content that other attendees are presenting, in order to establish your authority and build relationships.

Step 5: Keep an Eye on Your Progress and Results

Last but not least, it is imperative that you keep track of the outcomes of your collaborative efforts and make necessary adjustments to your strategy. Tracking engagement metrics, such as views and clicks, as well as conversion metrics, such as leads and revenue, can be done with the help of the analytics tools provided by LinkedIn.

Make adjustments to your strategy for working together based on the insights that you glean from the data collected by your analytics. For instance, if you notice that certain types of collaborations are generating more engagement than others, you should modify your collaboration strategy so that it focuses more on the types of collaborations that are generating the most engagement.

In a nutshell, the ability to collaborate on LinkedIn is indispensable for developing relationships and fostering the expansion of businesses. You can connect and collaborate with other businesses and professionals in your industry by joining relevant groups, working together on content creation, using LinkedIn Company Pages, attending LinkedIn events, and monitoring your results. You can also establish yourself as a thought leader in your industry by participating in LinkedIn events.

# Chapter 18: Mastering LinkedIn Video - Best Practices for Creating and Sharing Video Content on the Platform

O n LinkedIn, using video content to engage with your audience is becoming an increasingly common trend as well as an effective way to do so. You can produce and distribute high-quality video content on LinkedIn by making use of the platform's video features, such as native video and LinkedIn Live. This will allow you to increase user engagement, as well as establish your credibility and authority on the platform.

In this chapter, we will discuss the best practices for producing video content to share on LinkedIn and share it with others.

First, determine your video marketing strategy.

Establishing your video strategy should be the first thing you do. Which subjects do you plan to discuss in your videos, and what sort of point do you want to make clear to viewers?

Utilize the search tools provided by LinkedIn to locate pertinent topics and keywords, and then incorporate these discoveries into your video marketing strategy. Be sure to identify your target audience, and then cater your videos to the interests of that audience as well as the challenges they face.

The second step is to produce videos of a high quality.

It is absolutely necessary to produce videos of a high quality if you want to engage with your audience on LinkedIn and establish your credibility and authority in your field. Make sure that your videos have a great look and sound by using high-quality equipment, such as a camera and microphone that are designed for professionals.

Make your videos more interesting to watch and share with others by incorporating visual aids like slides or still images. You should keep your videos brief and to the point, and you should use the video editing tools that LinkedIn provides in order to edit and improve your videos before you share them.

Step 3: Distribute Your Video Content

It is essential to distribute your videos in order to communicate with your intended audience and increase engagement. You can upload your videos directly to the platform by utilizing LinkedIn's native video feature, or you can make use of LinkedIn Live to broadcast live video to your audience.

If you want users to watch your video, you need to make sure to include an interesting headline and description. You can make your videos more discoverable on LinkedIn by using the tagging feature to add tags that are pertinent to the videos. Users who are searching for specific topics will find your videos more easily.

The fourth step is to interact with the audience.

It is essential to build relationships, establish your credibility and authority, and establish your online presence as an authority on LinkedIn by engaging with your audience. Quickly respond to people's comments and messages, and get involved in the conversations taking place in LinkedIn groups.

Make use of the messaging tools provided by LinkedIn in order to connect with other thought leaders in your field and begin a conversation with them. If you want to reach a larger audience with your video content, you should share it on other social media platforms, such as Facebook or Twitter.

Step 5: Keep an Eye on Your Progress and Results

In conclusion, it is essential to monitor the results of your video content and modify your strategy in accordance with those findings. Tracking engagement metrics, such as views and clicks, as well as conversion metrics, such as leads and revenue, can be done with the help of the analytics tools provided by LinkedIn.

Make adjustments to your video content strategy in light of the insights gained from analyzing the data collected by your analytics platform. For instance, if you notice that particular categories of videos are generating more engagement than others, you should modify your video content strategy to place a greater emphasis on the categories of videos that fall into those categories.

In a nutshell, the use of video content is an effective method for engaging with one's audience on LinkedIn. You can create and share high-quality video content that increases engagement, establishes your credibility and authority on the platform, and drives engagement by defining your video strategy, creating high-quality videos, sharing your videos, engaging with your audience, and monitoring your results.

# Chapter 19: LinkedIn for Nonprofits - How Charities and Nonprofit Organizations Can Use LinkedIn to Drive Donations and Support

---

Nonprofit and charitable organizations can use LinkedIn as a powerful platform to increase awareness of their causes, drive donations, and build partnerships with other nonprofits and charitable organizations as well as individuals. By taking advantage of features on LinkedIn such as groups, company pages, and targeted advertising, nonprofit organizations are able to raise their profile in the community and communicate with a larger pool of prospective donors.

In this chapter, we will discuss different ways that nonprofit organizations can benefit from using LinkedIn.

Create a company page on LinkedIn as the first step.

The first thing you should do is establish a company page on LinkedIn for your charitable organization. Make use of your company page to communicate industry news and engage with other companies and individuals operating within your sector.

Utilize the analytics tools provided by LinkedIn to keep track of how users interact with your company page and make any necessary adjustments to your marketing approach. For instance, if you notice that particular categories of content are generating more engagement than others, you should modify your content strategy so that it focuses more on the categories of content that are generating the most engagement.

## Step 2: Join Relevant Groups

Joining groups that are pertinent to your search is essential if you want to find other nonprofits and potential donors on LinkedIn and connect with them. Utilize the search tools provided by LinkedIn to locate groups that are pertinent to your cause or mission, and then join these groups to take part in discussions and share your knowledge with others.

Be sure to add something of value to the conversation by discussing your own experiences and viewpoints, as well as taking an interest in the posts made by other users. Make use of the messaging tools provided by LinkedIn in order to connect with other users who are part of the group and begin a conversation with them.

## Step 3: Leverage Targeted Advertising

On LinkedIn, targeted advertising is a powerful tool that can be used to reach a larger audience of potential supporters. Make use of the advertising platform that LinkedIn provides in order to develop targeted advertisements that can reach users according to their job title, company, or interests.

You should make sure to create compelling ad copy and visuals that resonate with your target audience and communicate the mission and values of your nonprofit organization. Utilize the analytics tools that LinkedIn provides in order to keep track of how well your advertisements are performing and make any necessary adjustments to their targeting or messaging.

Participate in events hosted by LinkedIn. This is the fourth step.

It is absolutely necessary to take part in LinkedIn events in order to establish relationships with other charitable organizations and to work together with potential donors. Make use of the events feature on LinkedIn to locate events that are pertinent to your interests, such as webinars or conferences, and then participate in these events to network with other attendees.

Make use of the messaging tools provided by LinkedIn in order to connect with other attendees and begin a conversation with them. Be sure to share your own insights and perspectives, as well as engage with the content that other attendees are presenting, in order to establish your authority and build relationships.

Encourage employee advocacy as the fifth step.

A powerful strategy for amplifying the message of your nonprofit organization and reaching a wider audience on LinkedIn is to encourage employee advocacy. Encourage your staff members to share the latest updates and content from your nonprofit organization on their personal LinkedIn profiles, and provide them with resources, such as sample social media posts or graphics, to make it easier for them to share this information with others.

Always keep a close eye on how well your employee advocacy program is doing, and make any necessary adjustments to its approach. For instance, if you notice that particular categories of content are generating more engagement than others, you should modify your content strategy so that it focuses more on the categories of content that are generating the most engagement.

In a nutshell, nonprofits and charitable organizations can build partnerships with other organizations and individuals, increase their visibility in the community, and increase the amount of donations they receive by using the powerful platform that is LinkedIn. Nonprofit organizations can increase their visibility and reach a wider audience of potential supporters by encouraging employee advocacy, participating in LinkedIn events, creating a LinkedIn company page for their organization, joining relevant groups, utilizing targeted advertising, and creating a targeted advertising campaign.

# Chapter 20: The Future of LinkedIn Marketing - Trends, Predictions, and Strategies for Staying Ahead of the Curve

Because LinkedIn is a platform that is always undergoing change, staying one step ahead of the competition is absolutely necessary for achieving success with LinkedIn marketing. The platform is continually expanding and developing, and as a result, new marketing trends and strategies are emerging that are causing businesses and professionals to rethink their approach to marketing on LinkedIn.

In this chapter, we will discuss some of the trends and predictions for the future of LinkedIn marketing, as well as strategies for staying one step ahead of the competition in this space.

1. The Personalization of Everything

Personalization is a growing trend in LinkedIn marketing, as businesses and professionals seek to tailor their content and messaging to the particular needs and interests of their target audience. One way to accomplish this is through the use of LinkedIn Answers, which are questions and answers submitted by other users. The term "personalization" can refer to a wide range of practices, such as the deployment of targeted advertising and the production of landing pages and content that are specifically tailored to specific subsets of your audience.

Focus on developing a profound understanding of your target audience and making extensive use of data to personalize your content and messaging in order to stay one step ahead of the competition. Utilize the analytics tools that LinkedIn provides to keep track of how well your content is performing and adjust your strategy accordingly.

Trend 2: Video Content

Because companies and professionals want to engage their audience on LinkedIn with compelling and informative video content, the use of video content is becoming increasingly popular on the platform. Video can be utilized for a wide variety of purposes, including but not limited to employee profiles, product demonstrations, and thought leadership content videos.

Investing in high-quality video equipment and developing a video content strategy that is in line with your company's goals and the people you want to attract will keep you one step ahead of the competition. You can share your video content with your audience by using the native video and LinkedIn Live features that are available on LinkedIn.

Trend 3: LinkedIn Stories

The LinkedIn Stories feature is a relatively new addition to the platform, and it gives users the ability to share brief video and photo updates with their networks that disappear after a set amount of time. At this time, only a select few LinkedIn users have access to the Stories feature; however, it is anticipated that in the near future, more users will have access to this feature.

Experiment with LinkedIn Stories and investigate how this feature can be used to engage with your audience and share genuine, behind-the-scenes updates about your company or brand so that you can stay one step ahead of the competition. Doing so will help you stay one step ahead of the curve.

The fourth trend is purpose-driven marketing and social responsibility in business.

On LinkedIn, social responsibility and purpose-driven marketing are becoming increasingly important as businesses and professionals seek to align their marketing efforts with their values and make a positive impact in the world. LinkedIn is a platform that connects professionals and businesses around the world.

Focus on developing a powerful brand purpose and effectively communicating your company's values and social responsibility initiatives to your target audience if you want to stay one step ahead of the competition. Make use of LinkedIn's company pages and advertising features to disseminate the messaging that is purpose-driven to the audience that you have chosen.

In conclusion, the future of LinkedIn marketing is ever-changing, and in order to stay one step ahead of the competition, one needs an in-depth understanding of the most recent marketing trends and strategies. Businesses and professionals can stay ahead of the curve and drive success on the platform by placing an emphasis on personalization, video content, LinkedIn Stories, and social responsibility. Utilize the analytics tools provided by LinkedIn to keep track of how well your content is performing, make any necessary adjustments to your strategy, and play around with new features and trends in order to maintain your position at the forefront of LinkedIn marketing.

# About the Publisher

Accepting manuscripts in the most categories. We love to help people get their words available to the world.

Revival Waves of Glory focus is to provide more options to be published. We do traditional paperbacks, hardcovers, audio books and ebooks all over the world. A traditional royalty-based publisher that offers self-publishing options, Revival Waves provides a very author friendly and transparent publishing process, with President Bill Vincent involved in the full process of your book. Send us your manuscript and we will contact you as soon as possible.

Contact: Bill Vincent at rwgpublishing@yahoo.com